HEREDITY

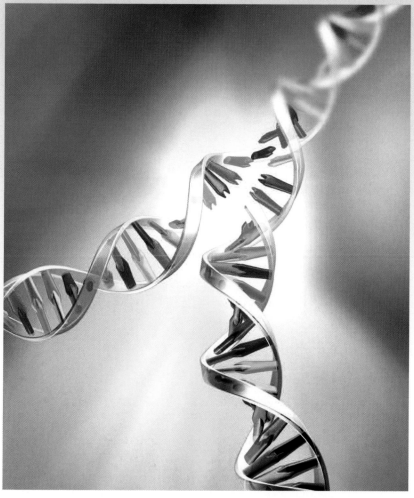

Darlene R. Stille
Contributing author: Carol Ryback

Consultant: Suzy Gazlay, M.A.,
science curriculum resource teacher

Please visit our web site at: www.garethstevens.com
For a free color catalog describing Gareth Stevens Publishing's list
of high-quality books, call 1-800-542-2595 (USA)
or 1-800-387-3178 (Canada).

Library of Congress Cataloging-in-Publication Data

Stille, Darlene R.
    Heredity / Darlene Stille. — North American ed.
      p. cm. — (Gareth Stevens vital science: life science)
    Includes bibliographical references and index.
    ISBN-13: 978-0-8368-8439-5 — ISBN-10: 0-8368-8439-6 (lib. bdg.)
    ISBN-13: 978-0-8368-8448-7 — ISBN-10: 0-8368-8448-5 (softcover)
    1. Heredity—Juvenile literature.   I. Title.
QH437.5.S752   2008
576.5—dc22   2007021476

This edition first published in 2008 by
Gareth Stevens Publishing
A Weekly Reader® Company
1 Reader's Digest Road
Pleasantville, NY 10570-7000 USA

Q2a Media editor: Honor Head
Q2a Media design, illustrations, and image search: Q2a Media
Q2a Media cover design: Q2a Media

Gareth Stevens editor: Carol Ryback
Gareth Stevens art director: Tammy West
Gareth Stevens graphic designer: Dave Kowalski
Gareth Stevens production: Jessica Yanke
Gareth Stevens science curriculum consultant: Suzy Gazlay, M.A.

Photo credits: Colin & Linda McKie / Shutterstock: half title, Kenneth Sponsler: 11, Mauro
Fermariello / SPL: 14, Andrew Syred / SPL: 19, Christian Darkin: 21, Pasieka / SPL: 25,
Ed Young / Agstock / SPL: 29, H. Raguet / Eurelios / SPL: 32, Tom Pantages / Phototake Inc: 35,
Ross Durant / Foodpix: 37, Gusto Gusto / SPL: 38, Karen Kasmauski / CORBIS: 41, Scott Bauer
/ ARS / USDA: 43.

Printed in the United States of America

1 2 3 4 5 6 7 8 9 11 10 09 08 07

Contents

1 Traits: Acquired and Inherited

Mendel and His Peas

The story of genetic science began in the middle of the nineteenth century. In what is now the Czech Republic, Austrian monk Gregor Johann Mendel experimented with pea plants. Through his experiments, Mendel discovered the laws of heredity.

Tiffany has wonderful manners. She always says "Please" and "Thank you." She is very respectful when talking to adults, classmates, and friends. In addition to her social skills, Tiffany also has excellent table manners.

Tiffany's parents are responsible for all of her social traits, or characteristics. They taught her to be polite, respectful, and to have good manners. Social characteristics, such as good manners, are acquired, or learned. Tiffany will not naturally pass her good manners along to her own children. Her children will need to learn about good manners, just as she did.

Tiffany is short, has dark, curly hair, and brown eyes. She had no choice about any of her physical

Offspring resemble their parents and each other because of inherited characteristics.

characteristics. All of them came from her parents. Physical characteristics, such as height and eye color, are inherited. They cannot be acquired by learning or any other means.

You can see examples of acquired and inherited traits in other animals. A new puppy must be trained. It must learn to come, sit, and stay. These are acquired traits. When the puppy grows up, it cannot pass these acquired obedience traits to its offspring. Coat color and ear length of the puppy occur naturally, however. The puppy inherits those physical characteristics from its parents.

Plants display only inherited characteristics. A climbing rose bush on a garden fence may produce red, white, or pink flowers. The color of the blossoms is an inherited trait. The roses do not "learn" to be red, pink, or white. Rose bushes and other plants that climb are not "taught" to climb. A plant cannot "learn." It simply attaches to whatever is nearby. A "climbing" plant climbs because its parents could.

Genes

Physical traits pass from parent animals and plants to their offspring through genes. Tiffany got the genes for her hair and eye color from her parents. Likewise, a puppy gets its long legs, stocky build, or pug nose from its parents. Genes also determine flower color, tree height, and leaf shape.

Nearly every cell of every living organism contains a complete set of genes for that organism. Genes are made of DNA (deoxyribonucleic acid). DNA determines what an organism looks like and how it develops.

Genes, made of DNA, are found on chromosomes.

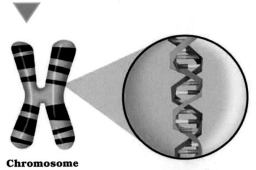

Chromosome

DNA

Genes at Work

Every cell is basically a tiny chemical factory. Genes tell that cell which chemicals to produce. The chemicals made by a cell determine its job. Some animal cells develop into muscle, nerve, or bone cells. Other cells help form organs, such as the stomach, liver, or skin. The genes of plant cells direct cells to form leaves, stems, or flowers.

An organism passes its genes to offspring during reproduction. Traits that pass from a parent to its offspring are called inherited traits. In order to understand how that happens, you must first learn how cells work.

Cell Division

All living things are made of cells. As an organism grows, new cells are created. Cells also wear out or die and need to be replaced. A process called cell division creates new cells. Cell division begins in an area of a cell called the

How Cells Know What To Do

Animals and plants may contain billions of cells. Each cell has a special job. Most cells also contain a complete set of genes. How does a cell know what to do? The secret is that only some of the genes in a cell are "turned on." In a bone cell, for example, only the genes that can make bone cells are turned on. In a plant leaf, only the genes that make leaf cells are turned on.

nucleus. The nucleus acts as a command center for the cell.

Most of the time, genes exist as irregular lumps of material called chromatin. Chromatin is found inside each nucleus. The chromatin changes shape only when a cell is about to divide. At that time, the chromatin forms into long structures called chromosomes.

7

Cell Without a Nucleus

All cells have a nucleus, except for red blood cells. Very young red blood cells (RBCs) do have a nucleus, however. The nucleus disappears as the RBC matures. By the time an RBC enters the bloodstream, it no longer has a nucleus. The RBC cannot reproduce itself.

Different animals and plants have different numbers of chromosomes in their cells. Dog cells, for example, have 39 pairs of chromosomes, or 78 in all. Human cells have 23 pairs of chromosomes, or a total of 46. Sperm and egg cells do not have the same number of chromosomes as other body cells. Human sperm and egg cells have only 23 chromosomes each.

There are two types of cell division. Both begin in the nucleus. The type of cell

Cell division that produces new eggs or sperm is a process called meiosis.

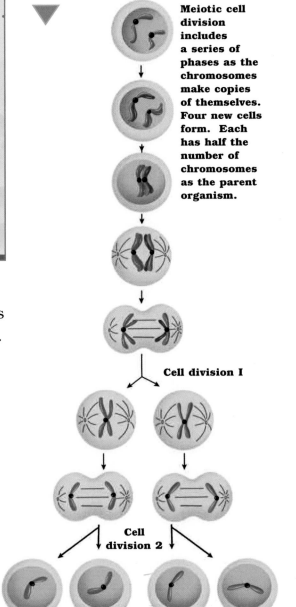

Meiotic cell division includes a series of phases as the chromosomes make copies of themselves. Four new cells form. Each has half the number of chromosomes as the parent organism.

Cell division I

Cell division 2

Cells that form by meiosis have half the normal number of chromosomes for that organism.

division that occurs in most cells is called mitosis. During mitosis, a cell's chromosomes make copies of themselves. This process happens in a series of steps, called phases. Eventually, the original cell divides into two new cells. Each new cell ends up with a full set of chromosomes. Any cell with a full set of chromosomes is also called a somatic cell. The new cell is an exact copy of the original cell.

Egg and sperm cells are created through a different type of cell division, called meiosis. Cells created through meiosis end up with a half set of chromosomes. As a result, egg and sperm cells have only half the number of genes of other cells. They are also called haploid cells.

When an egg and sperm cell join, they do not form two cells. Each is a haploid cell. They unite to form one new cell, which is a diploid cell. From that one cell, a new organism with a full set of

When Cells Divide

Some cells, such as hair and skin cells, divide almost constantly to replace dead cells. Other cells do not divide very often. Brain cells seldom divide.

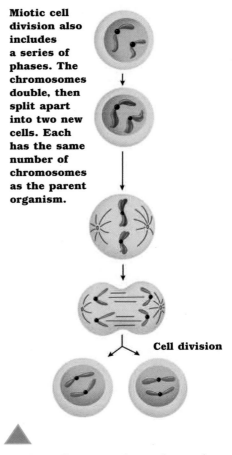

Miotic cell division also includes a series of phases. The chromosomes double, then split apart into two new cells. Each has the same number of chromosomes as the parent organism.

Cell division

Body cells reproduce through a process called mitosis.

9

Other Means of Reproduction

Not all organisms reproduce using egg and sperm cells. Bacteria and other one-celled organisms do not produce egg and sperm cells. They reproduce by binary fission. This process is similar to mitosis. The chromosomes in the cell duplicate. A wall forms, and the cell divides in half. The two new cells are genetically identical.

Yeast reproduce by budding. The nucleus in the yeast cell divides. A bubble forms in the yeast's cell wall. A new nucleus passes into the bubble, which splits away.

Some plants also reproduce without the help of another plant. For example, a tulip bulb can grow new bulbs to spread throughout a garden. The bulbs can be separated and replanted. Each grows into a new plant. Each tulip is a copy of the original plant.

chromosomes and genes can grow. It is how you began. Half of your genes came from your mother's egg cell. The other half came from your father's sperm cell.

A new organism has a new set of chromosomes, so each new organism also has its own unique mix of genes. As that new cell divides again and again, a new organism grows. Some of the traits of the offspring might have come from the mother, others from the father. This is why every organism, from people to plants, resembles its parents. Yet each offspring is different from every other.

🔑 Pronunciation Key:

acquired (*a-KWIRED*)
binary fission
   (BYE-nah-ree FIH-shun)
chromatin (*KROHM-a-tin*)
chromosome (*KROHM-a-sohm*)
meiosis (*my-OH-sis*)
nucleus (*NEW-klee-us*)

2 Genes and Heredity

We know that Tiffany has brown eyes. Her brother, Derek, has blue eyes. Tiffany has dark, curly hair. Derek's hair is a lighter brown. People often say, however, that Tiffany and Derek have noses that are the same shape.

Like Tiffany and Derek, the offspring in a family often share some physical characteristics. That happens because they may have inherited some of the same genes from their parents.

Identical twins have identical genes.

Two sisters, two brothers, or even a brother and a sister from the same family may look amazingly similar. At the same time, each child has his or her own unique appearance. Some identical twins, however, are nearly impossible to tell apart. They have exactly the same genes.

Mixing It Up

Family members look alike and yet different because of genetic variation. Genetic variation occurs when genes get mixed up during reproduction. Genes can get mixed up during several different phases of meiosis. The mix-up can occur when groups of genes swap places on the chromosomes. This kind of mixing-up is called crossing over.

Other times, parts of chromosomes break off during meiosis. When the chromosomes reform, groups of genes end up in different places from where they started.

Genes can also trade places during another phase of meiosis. The gene trade may happen as chromosomes split a second time. Each pair of chromosomes might separate independently. Genes that were usually together end up in different cells. This

Genes can cross over to a different location on a different chromosome during meiosis.

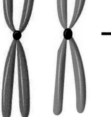

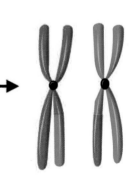

Two chromosomes   **Duplication**   **Crossing over**   **New chromosomes**

kind of mixing up is called random assortment.

Mutant Genes

A gene can change because of a mutation. A mutation is like a genetic mistake. For some reason, the order of the genes gets switched around. A mutation can produce a brand-new trait in an offspring. Sometimes, a genetic mutation causes problems in an offspring.

Genes can also trade places from generation to generation. You are a different generation from your parents. Your parents are a different generation from your grandparents. Your grandparents also had parents, and so on. It can often take a long time for genes to shift from generation

Possibilities

Genetic scientists, or geneticists, estimate that each human egg or sperm cell can carry eight million possible gene combinations. For this reason, each baby born is a unique individual. He or she has a set of genes that has never existed before and never will again. The only exception to this rule is in the case of identical twins.

to generation. Every living thing is a mixture of random genes from others that lived before them. Very often, a characteristic will skip a generation or two. That means your gene for body height or hair color may have come from one of your grandparents or even one of your great-grandparents! This is why it is possible for two of three sisters to have straight, dark hair, while the third has blond, curly hair.

🔦 Pronunciation Key:

allele (*ah-LEEL*)
geneticist (je-NEH-ti-syst)

Inheriting Color

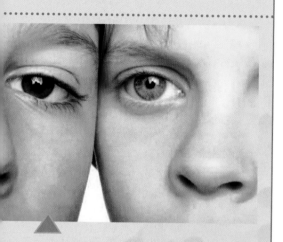

Eye color depends upon the combination of inherited alleles.

Human eye and hair color are inherited characteristics. Eye color is determined by the combination of alleles inherited from both your mother and father. Likewise, several genes on different chromosomes determine your hair color. Several alleles or several genes on different chromosomes are often involved in determining a trait. These genes have complicated inheritance patterns.

Alleles: Two or more forms of one gene

There is another reason that Tiffany and Derek have different characteristics. They each inherited different forms of the same gene. One set came from each parent.

In fact, all organisms that begin with an egg and a sperm inherit a mixed set of genes. Geneticists know that some genes have a sort of "home address." Such genes always appear at the same place on a certain chromosome. For instance, geneticists know which human chromosome contains the genes for eye color. A specific area on that chromosome can contain several combinations of gene pairs. These gene pairs are called alleles.

Different alleles can produce different effects. For example, pea plants have alleles that determine plant height. One set of alleles produces tall plants. Another set of alleles produces short plants.

3 Dominant and Recessive Genes

Alleles of a gene can be either dominant or recessive. Dominant means stronger. It has more influence on the offspring. If an offspring inherits one dominant allele and one recessive allele, the dominant trait will show up. For example, in pea plants, the allele for height is dominant.

The allele that produces a short plant is recessive. A pea plant with one dominant and one recessive allele will be tall.

Geneticists use a kind of shorthand to indicate alleles. They use a capital letter to indicate the dominant allele.

The allele that determines plant flower color appears in the same location on each chromosome.

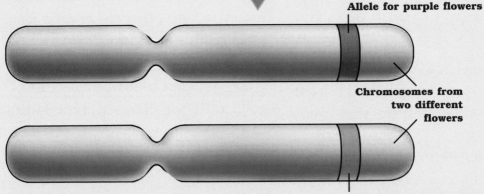

Allele for purple flowers

Chromosomes from two different flowers

Allele for white flowers

For example, tallness is shown as "T." The recessive allele is marked by a lowercase letter, so "t" indicates shortness.

The alleles for dominant and recessive traits can combine three ways. Two dominant alleles can be inherited. Two recessive alleles can be inherited. The third combination is one dominant and one recessive

Alike and Different Alleles

Geneticists have ways to identify pairs of alleles that are alike or different. Alleles that are alike, such as "TT" or "tt," are homozygous. The prefix "homo" means "same." Alleles that are different, such as "Tt," are heterozygous. The prefix "hetero" means different. "Zygous" refers to zygote. A zygote is the cell that forms when a sperm and egg unite as a new organism.

allele. Consider the pea plants. The shorthand for two dominant alleles is "TT." The shorthand for two recessive alleles is "tt." The shorthand for a pea plant with one of each is "Tt." The set of genes and alleles that an organism inherits is called its genotype.

Gene Expression

The genotype of the dominant allele is always stronger than the recessive version. A pea plant with the genotype "TT" will be tall. A pea plant with the genotype "Tt" will also be tall. A pea plant with the genotype "tt" will be short. A recessive characteristic can only appear if two recessive alleles are inherited.

The physical appearance of an individual is called its phenotype. The phenotype for pea plants with either the "TT" or "Tt" genotype is tall. The phenotype for pea plants with the "tt" genotype is short. Genotype determines an individual's phenotype.

The Odds of Inheritance

Parents who are expecting a baby often wonder what the baby will look like. Will the baby have blue eyes or brown eyes? Will the baby grow up to be tall like her father or short like her mother?

Special math laws are used in genetic science. These laws are called the laws of probability. Probability laws govern the chances, or odds, of offspring inheriting a certain trait. Geneticists use a diagram called a Punnett Square to predict the genotype of a trait. A Punnett Square is a set of boxes. The possible allele combinations are listed along the top and sides of a Punnett Square.

A Punnett Square of the possible allele combinations.

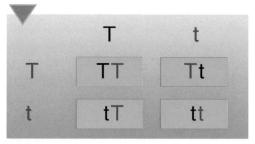

A Punnett Square for the height of a pea plant appears below. The genotype for the "male" plant, genotype "Tt," appears at the top. The genotype for the "female" plant appears along the left side. As you can see, each parent plant has the same genotype for height.

The four lower right squares show the possible gene combinations that can occur. Notice that every offspring has three chances to inherit genes with the dominant set of alleles. Any new plant with either the "TT" or "Tt" genotype will have the "tall" phenotype. This Punnett Square also shows that each offspring could also inherit the "tt" genotype instead. The odds for producing a short plant from these parents are one in four. A geneticist would list the probability law for this result as a mathematical shorthand called a ratio. The ratio for producing a short plant from these parent plants is written as 1:4. Each offspring has only a 25 percent chance of being short.

Genes and Gender

Special chromosomes determine the sex, or gender, of an organism. In humans, the sex chromosomes are called X and Y chromosomes. Males have one X and one Y chromosome. The genotype for a human male is "XY." Females have two X chromosomes. The genotype for a human female is "XX."

Eggs carry only X chromosomes. Sperm can carry either an X or a Y chromosome. When a sperm with a Y chromosome joins with an egg, the offspring will be male (XY). When a sperm carrying an X chromosome joins with an egg, the offspring will be female (XX).

The X and Y chromosomes also carry genes for other characteristics. These other genes are called sex-linked genes. The X chromosome is much larger than the Y chromosome. Geneticists estimate that the smaller Y chromosome carries only about 25 sex-linked genes. The X chromosome carries about one thousand sex-linked genes.

Some sex-linked genes can cause genetic, or inherited, health disorders. If a male inherits the recessive form of a sex-linked gene from his mother, he will likely develop that disorder. The two X chromosomes of a female may contain one dominant gene and one recessive gene. The dominant gene will rule. The female will not develop the disorder. A female must inherit a recessive gene from both of her parents to develop

---

🔑 Pronunciation Key:

genotype (*GEE-noh-TYPE*)

hemophilia (*HEE-mo-FEE-lee-ah*)

phenotype (*FEE-noh-TYPE*)

zygote (*ZEYE-goat*)

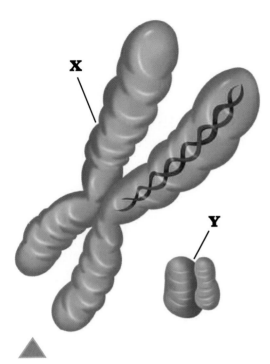

The X and Y chromosomes carry sex-linked genes.

Reginald Punnett

English geneticist Reginald C. Punnett (1875–1967) invented the Punnett Square in the early 1900s. He used the device to explain why recessive traits did not simply disappear over time.

the health problem. This female can, however, pass either a dominant or recessive gene to her own children. Male offspring with the recessive gene will always develop the genetic disorder. Female offspring with the recessive gene will only develop the disorder if the X chromosome of that offspring's father also carries the recessive gene.

Royal Genes

One of the most famous examples of recessive genes passing between families occurred in Europe. Queen Victoria ruled the United Kingdom from 1837 to 1901. She and her husband, Albert, had nine children. Victoria did not know she carried the gene for hemophilia. Hemophilia is a disease that causes problems with blood clotting. Someone with hemophilia can bleed to death from even a small cut or from internal bleeding. Queen Victoria passed the allele for hemophilia to two of her daughters and one of her sons. The disease usually develops only in males.

Queen Victoria's children married members of other royal European families. In some cases, one royal first cousin married another royal first cousin. A royal half-brother might have married his royal half-sister. An older royal uncle, prince, or former king might marry his young niece. In this way, the recessive allele passed to children of royal families in Spain, Germany, and Russia. Some of them developed hemophilia.

Other genetic diseases include cystic fibrosis and sickle cell anemia. Cystic fibrosis is a lung disease. Sickle cell anemia is a blood disorder. As you have seen, a recessive gene can cause a disease. It can also affect how long that person or organism lives. People who have hemophilia, cystic fibrosis, or sickle cell anemia

often do not survive as long as someone without such a genetic disorder.

Sickle Cell anemia

Sickle cell anemia gets its name from the abnormal shape of red blood cells. Normal red blood cells are round, like car tires. They carry oxygen throughout the body. Normal red blood cells are flexible. They can squeeze through the tiniest blood vessels in tissues and organs.

Sickled cells are curved and stiff. They plug up small blood vessels and keep oxygen from getting to all body cells. Without oxygen, body cells suffer damage. Sickle cell disease develops when a child inherits abnormal hemoglobin alleles from each parent.

A parent with one normal allele and one abnormal allele has sickle cell trait. That adult has no symptoms, but can pass the abnormal allele on to offspring. A blood test can determine if a parent has

4 DNA: The Master Molecule

We already know that genes pass traits to offspring and direct the workings of every animal or plant cell. We also know they are made of a long molecule called DNA, or deoxyribonucleic acid. DNA is often called the "master molecule" of life. This master molecule holds the blueprint to how organisms develop—no matter if they are tiny, one-celled bacteria or the enormous blue whale.

The blue whale is not only the largest creature on Earth, it is also the loudest!

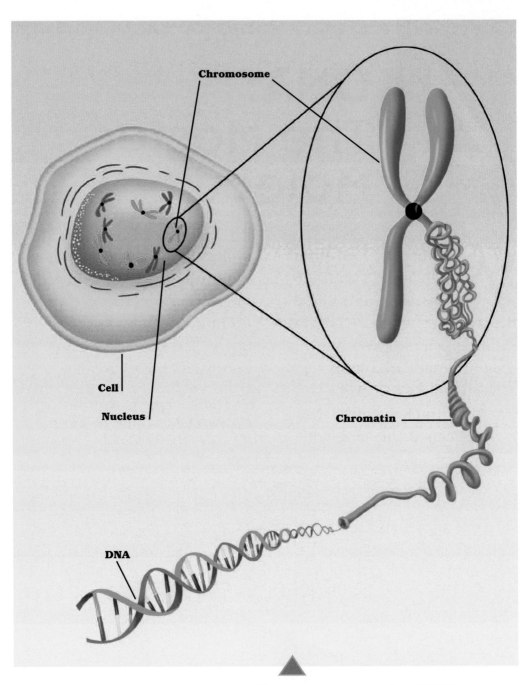

Chromosome

Cell

Nucleus

Chromatin

DNA

*Chromosomes, made of DNA,
transfer genes between generations.*

A DNA molecule is a long strand of genetic material. One strand of DNA can contain thousands of genes. Genes are sections on a DNA strand. The DNA that makes up a gene carries a code. The code tells each cell how to make a substance called a protein.

Every protein produced by a cell has a specific job. Some proteins direct cell structure and function as an organism grows. Other proteins, called hormones and enzymes, control cell metabolism.

The DNA Molecule

The master molecule of life looks like a long, twisted

🔑 Pronunciation Key:

adenine (EH-de-neen)
cytosine (SIGH-ti-seen)
deoxyribonucleic
(dee-OX-ee-RYE-boh-noo-KLEE-ick)
guanine (GWA-neen)
phosphates (FOS-fates)
thymine (THIGH-meen)

DNA As Évidence

Only identical twins share the same DNA code. All other people have a unique genetic makeup. Detectives, police, and other criminal investigators can use DNA codes to solve crimes. They collect materials, such as hair, blood, and skin, from a crime scene. Laboratory workers study the DNA samples. They compare DNA found at the crime scene with that of suspected criminals. If any DNA patterns match, the investigators have a better chance of proving that someone is guilty.

DNA can also help identify animals. Veterinarians can use DNA to identify a lost pet. U.S. Customs and Border Protection agents can use animal and plant DNA testing. The DNA can identify endangered animal or plant species that people are trying to bring into the country.

Solving the Mystery of DNA

Since the 1890s, scientists had thought that something like DNA existed. But they were not sure exactly how it worked. By the 1940s, scientists had a pretty good idea that DNA made up the genes. The first step toward understanding DNA was made by British chemist and molecular biologist Rosalind Franklin. She and her fellow worker, Maurice Wilkins, studied X-ray images of DNA. In 1953, American biologist James Watson and British biologist Francis Crick determined that DNA has the shape of a twisted ladder. They called this shape a "double helix." Watson, Crick, and Wilkins won the 1962 Nobel Prize in Physiology or Medicine for their discovery of the shape of DNA. They could not have been successful without the help of Franklin, who died in 1958.

ladder. The sides of the DNA ladder are made of chemicals called carbohydrates and phosphates. The "rungs" of the ladder are made of four chemical units called bases.

The bases are adenine (A), thymine (T), cytosine (C), and guanine (G). Every living organism is "built" from these four bases. They form pairs to make genes. What differs between genes is the order and number of pairs.

Adenine always pairs with thymine. Cytosine always pairs with guanine. The base pairs are arranged to form a DNA code. The DNA code is different for every organism. The entire DNA code for any animal or plant is called its genome.

DNA's ladder shape permits one body cell to divide to produce two body cells. When it is time for a cell to divide, the DNA ladder rungs pull completely apart. Each side of the ripped-apart ladder creates a duplicate of itself.

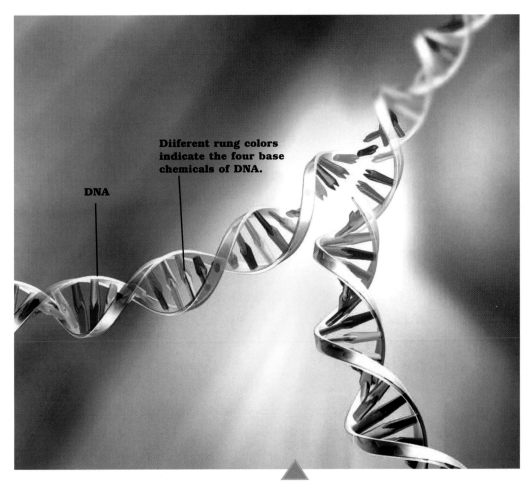

DNA

Diiferent rung colors indicate the four base chemicals of DNA.

The twisted-ladder-shape of DNA molecule is an efficient way to store an organism's genetic code.

The new DNA is identical to the original DNA. Again, A always pairs with T and C always pairs with G. Once the DNA has made an exact copy of itself, the cell divides.

A cell also uses its DNA as a pattern for making proteins used in bodily processes. Another cell chemical, called ribonucleic acid, or RNA, carries out this task. The main difference between DNA and RNA is found in the base pairs of these large molecules. Instead of thymine, RNA has a base

25

called uracil. To make a protein, only part of the DNA ladder—the section that holds the code for the exact protein needed—will "unzip" for duplication. RNA carries that protein code from the nucleus into the cytoplasm. Several cell organelles, including the endoplasmic reticulum and the ribosomes, are involved in manufacturing the protein.

Genetic Mutations

Genes do not always stay the same. Changes frequently occur in genes. Such changes are called mutations. Even a slight change in a gene changes which protein gets made. Sometimes, a change is harmful. Other times, a change is good. Most times, the result of a change in one gene makes no difference.

Mutations often occur during cell division. As the chromosomes are duplicating, several base pairs of a gene or even a complete gene may get left out. If genetic material crosses over to a different chromosome, it can cause a mutation that may or may not show up in that organism's phenotype—how it looks.

Some mutations occur in body cells as a part of normal metabolism. Cancer can develop with the mutation of one or more genes in body cells. Mutations that occur in body cells cannot be passed along to offspring. But genetic mutations that occur in sperm or egg cells can be passed along to offspring. Hemophilia, red-green color blindness, and sickle cell anemia are genetic disorders. They are caused by genetic mutations in sperm or egg cells.

Biologists have found several causes of mutations. Some mutations occur when the gene is being copied during cell division. Substances in the environment, such as dangerous chemicals and cigarette smoke, sometimes cause mutations.

Rays from the Sun can

cause mutations that lead to skin cancer.

Many changes probably occur in our DNA every day. But after a strand of DNA is copied, it goes through a kind of quality control. Cells contain special repair genes that can fix DNA errors. If an errors slips through, a mutation occurs.

Individuals with beneficial mutations often survive to reproduce. Sometimes, a mutant gene can help create a new breed. Over thousands of generations, a mutation may even cause an entirely new species to evolve.

Mutations can occur because of changes to a gene or chromosome.

DELETION

DUPLICATION

INVERSION (flipping of order)

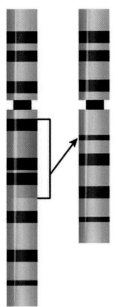

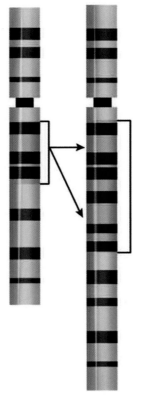

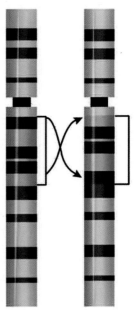

5 Genes and Medicine

Medical science is going through a sort of medical revolution because of our many genetic discoveries. We have new drugs, treatments, and even cures for diseases that once were always fatal (deadly). We can also alter, or change, some genes. This process is called genetic engineering.

Drugs from "Bugs"

One of the first uses of genetic engineering was for making new kinds of drugs. The drugs do not come directly from switching around genes of an organism, however. This process involves several steps.

To keep things simple, genetic engineers like to work with an organism that has only a few genes. Bacteria are simple organisms. Their DNA carries only a few genes. Geneticists also like to use bacteria, or "bugs," because it is easy to grow large batches of them.

Genetic engineers begin by studying a bacterium's DNA. They identify its genes and figure out the "job" of each. Next, they experiment with gene replacement techniques. Geneticists have learned how to put human genes into bacteria. These organisms are transgenically "engineered" bacteria. When

Genetic engineering research for farm crops may involve the use of DNA from large numbers of plants.

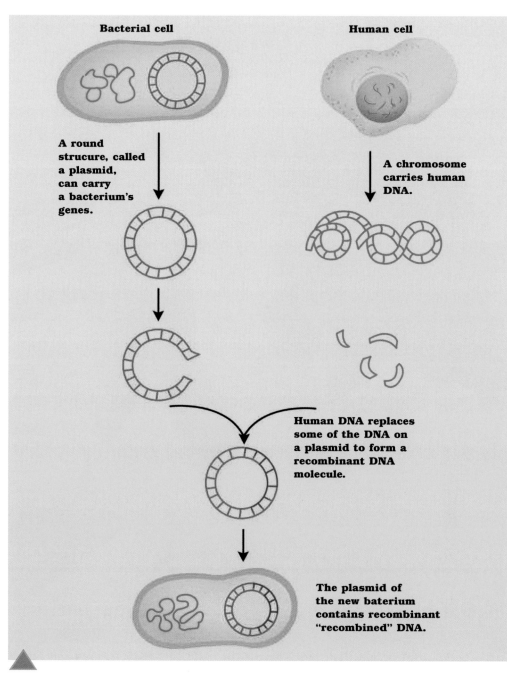

Bacterial cell

Human cell

A round strucure, called a plasmid, can carry a bacterium's genes.

A chromosome carries human DNA.

Human DNA replaces some of the DNA on a plasmid to form a recombinant DNA molecule.

The plasmid of the new baterium contains recombinant "recombined" DNA.

A bacterium can be genetically engineered to carry recombinant DNA.

these new bacteria reproduce, the resulting organisms will contain a human gene.

Like all living things, any bacteria—whether genetically engineered or not—will normally produce substances called by-products. For instance, sweat is a by-product of your metabolism. A bacterium that is genetically engineered to carry a human gene will produce a by-product that is different from its normal kind. Geneticists can use the new bacterial by-products to make the desired drugs.

The first drugs made from by-products of genetically engineered bacteria were marketed in 1982. Since then, many new drugs have been developed using genetic engineering techniques.

Genetic Testing

Geneticists can now identify some of the genes that cause diseases. They have developed blood tests to check for those genes. Doctors take a blood

sample. Special test methods reveal the "bad" genes.

Some couples undergo genetic testing before they have children. Genetic testing is important to couples who are concerned about passing a hereditary disease to their offspring. A couple might request such a test if either the man, woman, or a family member of either is a known carrier of a genetic disease.

Cystic fibrosis is a genetic disorder that causes major lung problems. Someone with cystic fibrosis has a hard time breathing. The disease causes lots of mucus to form in the lungs and other organs. Cystic fibrosis is a recessive disease. Only those offspring who inherit a recessive allele from both parents will develop the disease. Genetic testing of the parents can reveal if either carries the recessive gene allele for cystic fibrosis.

Some genetic diseases take many years to cause a health problem. In other words, a

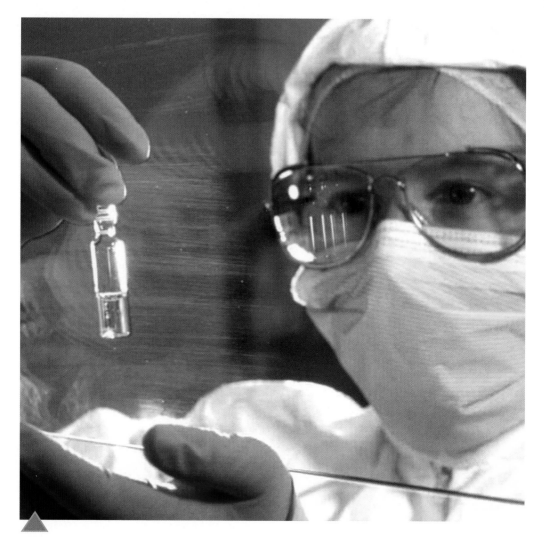

Genetic testing can help parents who carry recessive genes produce a healthy child.

person who appears healthy may carry a bad gene without knowing it. That person may not develop the genetically linked disease until he or she is ten, twenty, or thirty years old—or older. For instance, your uncle may have inherited the genes for heart problems, but he did not show any cardiac distress until he reached his mid-forties.

Genetic testing can help alert such people to possible health challenges in their future. For example, they might want to change their eating or exercise habits to help delay the onset of heart disease. Such lifestyle changes may not prevent the heart problem from developing, but they may at least lessen its effects.

Gene Therapy

Genetic researchers hope to someday routinely replace defective genes with healthy genes. They are developing "cut" and "paste" gene techniques. These treatments must not harm the patient. Researchers must be very careful with their genetic experiments. They do not want to cause more problems than they solve.

Gene Therapy

Gene therapy was first tried on two girls in 1990. The girls were four and nine years old. Their immune systems did not work properly. An inherited gene prevented the girls' bodies from fighting off germs. Researchers at the National Institutes of Health in Bethesda, Maryland, studied the girls' blood. They found a way to help the girls. Special cells in blood called white blood cells help fight germs. Researchers found a way to inject healthy genes into the girls' white blood cells. The girls were able to live normal lives. This gene therapy techinique was also used on newborn babies. Geneticists are still extremely cautious about using gene therapy. They realize that gene therapy is too new to use as a routine treatment in most cases.

6 Traits, Genes, and Agriculture

Cloning

Clones are two or more organisms with the same genetic makeup. They are common in nature. Bacteria, yeast, and simple animals, such as sponges, can easily clone themselves. Plants often produce clones. They develop when a piece of the parent plant, such a leaf, part of the root, or the "eye" of a potato, grows into a new plant. Clones can also be produced artificially.

For thousands of years, farmers have bred animals and plants with "good" genes. Back then, farmers did not realize they were practicing a kind of genetic engineering. They did not even know that there was such a thing as genes. They only knew that some animals and plants had desirable characteristics.

For example, a farmer may have owned some cows that gave a lot of milk but did not live very long. He may have also owned some bulls that lived long lives. The farmer could breed the bulls with the cows. What he was hoping for were long-lived offspring. He would want the female offspring (the cows) to produce a lot of milk and live a long time.

Food scientists can put new genes into some fruits and vegetables. For instance, they can produce tomatoes that grow larger and last longer on the supermarket shelf.

Farmers and gardeners also worked to breed better plants. Thousands of years ago, they learned to plant seeds from only the better-tasting wild plants. In the 1700s, they learned more about how plants reproduce. Someone figured out that pollen from one plant could fertilize another plant.

Experiments showed that people could use pollen to produce exactly the type of plants they wanted. For instance, they might have a strong corn plant that produced small ears. They might have another plant that didn't grow very well but produced large, sweet ears of corn. They used pollen from the strong plant to fertilize the weaker one. What they hoped to produce was a strong corn plant with large, sweet ears. They wanted the good traits to cross to the offspring of the parent plants. The deliberate transfer of genetic traits is called crossbreeding.

A plant or animal created by crossbreeding is called a hybrid. Farmers would gather plant hybrids with desirable traits, plant the seeds, and hope that most of the offspring would grow to produce more plants with those same desirable characteristics.

Such attempts to introduce desirable traits into animals and plants were not always successful. Crossbreeding did not always result in what the breeders wanted. It could also introduce undesirable traits. Most times, it took farmers years to produce the type of plant or animal with exactly the characteristics they desired.

Genetically Engineered Plants

In the late twentieth century, botanists, or plant scientists,

⚷ Pronunciation Key:

cytoplasm (*SIGH-toh-PLAH-sem*)
mitochondria
(*MIGH-toh-KAHN-dree-uh*)

learned how to speed up the process of producing better plants. They used genetic engineering techniques to insert a gene from another species into the DNA of a plant cell. Viruses—tiny living organisms—can carry genes between species. The new gene arrangement might make the plant resistant to (able to fight off) plant diseases. Plants created this way are called transgenic plants. Transgenic corn plants could grow crops that were resistant to bugs called corn weevils.

Seedless watermelons are genetically engineered fruit.

In the late 1930s, botanists began developing seedless watermelons. In order to produce these hybrid plants, they used genetic engineering techniques. It takes several plant generations to produce the desired fruit. It also takes a long time to gather enough of the two types of seeds required to produce profitable crops. All of this adds to the price of seedless watermelons.

Botanists use a chemical to produce plants whose fruit have seeds with twice as many chromosomes as normal. Those seeds are then planted near seeds with the normal number of chromosomes. Pollen from normal plants must pollinate the flowers of the genetically engineered plants with the double set of chromosomes. These genetically engineered plants have flowers that grow into seedless watermelons. Seedless watermelon plants are hybrids that cannot reproduce. They have no seeds from which to grow new plants!

37

Dolly the Cloned Sheep

Dolly the sheep was the first cloned mammal. Researcher Ian Wilmut helped develop cloning.

In 1996, genetic researchers in Scotland cloned a sheep named Dolly. The researchers started with a body cell from a six-year-old female sheep. They removed the DNA from the nucleus of that cell. It was not a sperm or egg cell, so the nucleus had a full set of chromosomes. The geneticists also removed the nucleus from an egg cell taken from a different sheep. They inserted the nucleus with the full set of chromosomes into the egg cell. The egg cell was placed into yet another sheep. This sheep was Dolly's birth mother. Dolly was not genetically related to her birth mother. Her DNA was an exact copy of the DNA found in her genetic mother.

Genetically Engineered Animals

In the 1970s, geneticists learned how to insert genes from one animal species into another species. An animal produced using this technique is called a transgenic animal. Mice were the first transgenic animals that were developed.

The researchers also learned how to make other transgenic animals, such as rabbits, sheep, and pigs. Researchers use transgenic laboratory animals to study what happens when genes from different species of animals combine.

Some transgenic animals can help us produce drugs. For example, drugs called clotting factors are used to treat hemophilia. Genes for making these drugs have been inserted into the genome of cows and other farm animals. The animals then produce the needed drugs in their milk. Researchers collect the milk from these transgenic animals. Then they remove the drugs to make medicines. Drugs made from the milk of farm animals might be used for treating burns, wounds, and some forms of cancer.

Mammals do not produce natural clones. Scottish researchers achieved a milestone in 1996 with the cloning of Dolly the sheep. She grew from one body cell of an adult sheep. It takes several steps to grow an animal this way.

Geneticists soon discovered that because Dolly's DNA came from a six-year-old cow, her DNA was genetically six years old when she was born. It made her age faster than expected. Dolly produced several offspring, which in turn reproduced. She died when she was only six-and-a-half years old. Dolly's life lasted only half as long as that of a normal sheep because of her "older" DNA.

7 Genetics and Ethical Issues

Career: Genetic Counselor

A genetic counselor helps people who have a genetic disorder deal with their problem. The counselor might offer advice on certain treatments or help people make decisions about future genetic testing. Some also help individuals to better cope with any diseases that develop. Usually, counselors work as part of a medical team.

Genetic science and technology holds many promises for the future. Such procedures may someday treat and even prevent certain illnesses. The proper use of genetic techniques must also follow ethical guidelines. "Ethical" means that the procedures are fair and will not purposely harm living creatures.

Many people worry that genetic information could be used against them. Questions arise about the privacy issues regarding storage and retrieval of genetic information. Who would have access to it? Would employers use such information to decide whether to hire someone? Would insurance companies refuse to sell insurance to someone whose genes might lead to health problems later in life?

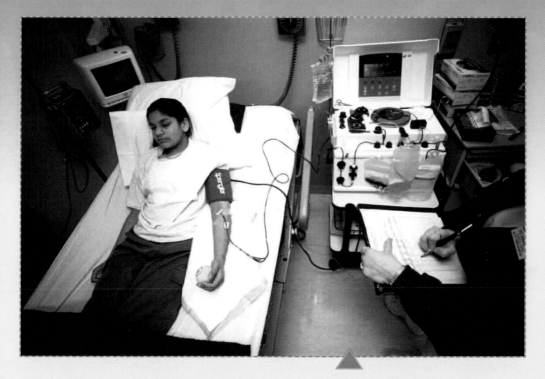

In 2003, the Human Genome Project, which "mapped" all the genes in the human body, was completed. Researchers identified the makeup and placement of many genes on human DNA. Scientists hope that one day they will have the tools to easily analyze someone's DNA. That way, they could predict the possible illnesses that person could develop. Doctors could take steps to prevent a health problem from developing.

Ashanti De Silva was four years old when she became the first human to receive gene therapy in 1990. Her doctors inserted new DNA into blood cells to replace her defective genes. She received the new genes through a blood transfusion.

Better Food?

Genetic technology in agriculture can produce crops that are easy to grow and highly nutritious. Genetically engineered crops that grow with little water or in poor soil could help feed people in many areas around the world.

Genetically altered crop plants are already available. Genetically altered soybeans are resistant to weed killers. Corn has also been genetically altered to boost resistance to certain insects.

People often disagree about whether or not genetic alterations are a good thing. They say that genes inserted into plants and animals go against nature. They fear that genetically altered foods could hold hidden dangers. They wonder if genetically engineered foods may cause severe allergic reactions in some people.

Others fear that changing the genes of plants and animals may cause brand-new problems in the future. For example, genetically altered insects may become impossible to control. Genetically altered weeds could become "superweeds" and wipe out natural plants or farm crops.

Keeping It Safe

Government agencies work to keep our food supply safe. The United States Food and Drug Administration (USDA) has special rules that govern genetically altered foods. It controls the use of genetically engineered plants and animals. Seed companies must carefully test genetically altered seeds before using them for food crops.

Genetic scientists will no doubt continue to make new discoveries. They will develop new genetic techniques and products. This knowledge can improve the health of people everywhere. It may also help feed everyone on the planet.

Human Genome Project

The entire set of genes in an organism is called its genome. In 1990, an international effort called the Human Genome Project began. Its goal was to completely map the human genome. A gene map is somewhat like a state map that shows every county, city, street, and building.

Geneticists study genetic "maps" to determine gene location.

The Human Genome Project created a list of the exact order of genes on human DNA. When it was completed, in 2003, scientists had a complete "map" of the human genome. The map was so detailed that it even listed the base pairs of each gene.

Information learned from the genome project is available to researchers all over the world. They want to learn as much as they can about every gene. They will use that information to determine what each does and its health effects.

Geneticists can also study the genome to determine the similarities and differences of genes from people around the world.

Researchers have mapped the genes of other species as well. In 2006, the United States government began to develop another program. It will create a map of the genes of several microorganisms, such as bacteria and viruses.

Scientists hope to develop new ways of using those microorganisms. Perhaps the new organisms could one day help us produce energy or clean up the environment.

Glossary

allele one of two genes in a pair contributed by parents

acquired a trait that is not inherited or passed on by genes; a learned trait

bacteria a single-celled microorganism

binary fission a splitting in half of an organism to create two new organisms without exchanging genetic material

base pairs two chemicals that bond to help form genes

carbohydrate a sugar or starch found in food that is metabolized for energy

clone an organism with the exact genome of its parent organism

chromatin loosely arranged genetic matter in the nucleus that forms into chromosomes during cell division

chromosomes thread-like genetic structures that form during cell division

crossing over to switch a location of a gene from one chromosome to another

cytoplasm the main, gel-like body of a cell

diploid a cell with a full set of chromosomes

DNA (deoxyribonucleic acid) the large molecule that makes up genes

egg a female sex cell

fertilize to join a male and female cell

gender an organism's sex

genes the basic units of heredity that pass between generations of organisms

gene therapy the process of replacing defective genes with desired or healthy genes

geneticists people who study genes and how they affect organisms

genome the complete set of genes in an organism

genotype the genetic makeup of an organism

haploid a cell with a single set of chromosomes; an egg or sperm cell

hemophilia a genetic disorder in which blood fails to clot properly

hybrid a plant or animal that results when parent organisms are mated, often in hopes of producing offspring with desired traits

inherit to pass a trait to offspring through genes

mutation a change in a gene

nucleus a structure that controls cell metabolism

phenotype the physical traits, such as color or height, evident in an organism

phosphates chemicals that help make up the backbone of DNA molecules

pollen dust-like grains of flowers that help the plants transfer genetic material

probability the mathematical chance, or the "odds," that an event will occur

protein a chemical produced by animal and plant cells to perform various functions

Punnett Square a device for estimating the probability of inheritance of dominant and recessive alleles

recessive allele a gene set that has no influence over an organism's phenotype

reproduction the production of a new "individual," be it a cell or a complete organism

sperm a male sex cell

trait a characteristic, such as eye or hair color

virus a microorganism that can cause disease

zygote an egg that has been fertilized by a sperm

For More Information

Books

Bedoyere, Camilla de la.
The Discovery of DNA. Milestones in Modern Science (series). World Almanac® Library (2006).

Dowswell, Paul.
Genetic Engineering.
21st-Century Issues (series).
World Almanac® Library (2004).

Fullick, Ann.
Inheritance and Selection.
Life Science, In-Depth (series).
Heinemann (2005).

Graham, Ian. *Genetics: The Study of Heredity.* Investigating Science (series). Gareth Stevens (2002).

Hamilton, Janet. *James Watson: Solving the Mystery of DNA*. Nobel Prize-Winning Scientists (series). Enslow Publishers (2004).

Hasan, Heather. *Mendel and the Laws of Genetics*, Rosen Publishing Group, 2005.

Pasachof, Naomi E. *Barbara McClintock: Genius of Science*. Great Minds of Science (series). Enslow Publishers (2006).

Web sites

www.genetics.gsk.com/kids /index_kids.htm

Explore GlaxoSmithKline's kids genetics pages.

www.genome.gov/glossary.cfm

Choose a word from the Human Genome Project's Talking glossary, then listen and learn!

www.pbs.org/opb/historydetectives/tec hniques/dna.html

Use DNA analysis to help solve historical mysteries.

www.niehs.nih.gov/kids/ genes/home.htm

Find simple information about DNA on this Web site.

www.dnaftb.org/dnaftb/

Watch an animated history about genetic sciences.

Index